Making

Shaking

Angela Aylmore

Heinemann
LIBRARY

www.heinemann.co.uk/library
Visit our website to find out more information about **Heinemann Library** books.

To order:
☎ Phone 44 (0) 1865 888066
▤ Send a fax to 44 (0) 1865 314091
▭ Visit the Heinemann Bookshop at www.heinemann.co.uk/library to browse our catalogue and order online.

First published in Great Britain by Heinemann Library, Halley Court, Jordan Hill, Oxford OX2 8EJ, part of Harcourt Education.

Heinemann is a registered trademark of Harcourt Education Ltd.
© Harcourt Education Ltd 2005.
First published in paperback in 2005.

Editorial: Kathy Peltan and Kate Bellamy
Design: Jo Hinton-Malivoire and Bigtop
Picture Research: Ruth Blair
Production: Severine Ribierre

Originated by Chroma Graphics (Overseas) Pte. Ltd
Printed and bound in China by South China Printing Company

ISBN 0 431 08824 1 (hardback)
09 08 07 06 05
10 9 8 7 6 5 4 3 2 1

ISBN 0 431 08829 2 (paperback)
09 08 07 06 05
10 9 8 7 6 5 4 3 2 1

British Library Cataloguing in Publication Data
Aylmore, Angela
Making Music: Shaking
786.8
A full catalogue record for this book is available from the British Library.

Acknowledgements
The publishers would like to thank the following for permission to reproduce photographs: Alamy pp. **8**, **16**, **18**; Corbis pp. **5a** (David Katzenstein), **13**; Getty Image p. **9** (Photodisc); Harcourt Education pp. **4a** (Gareth Boden), **4b**, **5b**, **6**, **7**, **10a**, **10b**, **11**, **12**, **14**, **15**, **17**, **19**, **20**, **21**, **22-23** (Tudor Photography).

Cover photograph of a boy shaking a rattle, reproduced with permission of Harcourt Education/Tudor Photography.

Every effort has been made to contact copyright holders of any material reproduced in this book. Any omissions will be rectified in subsequent printings if notice is given to the publishers.

The paper used to print this book comes from sustainable resources.

Contents

Let's make music!

We can make music by shaking!

Ben shakes his tambourine.

Ding!

Ring the bells!

5

Play the tambourine

Can you play the
tambourine?

Shake it gently.
Keep it **soft**.

tr-tr-tr-tr

6

tr–tr–tr–tr

Shake it hard.
Make it
loud.

Ding, dong bells

Can you play the bells?

Ding!

Dong!

8

You play a high note.

I will play a low note.

9

Make your own

Can you make a shaker?

Look at my shaker.

Look at my shaker.

chi-chi, chi-chi

chu-chu, chu-chu

Do they sound the same?

pitter,
patter

pitter,
patter

13

Music for a story

Let's use music to tell a story!

Eensy, weensy spider climbed up the waterspout.

Down came the rain and washed poor Eensy out.

Woosh!

15

What is it?

This is a sistrum. It comes from Egypt. It sounds like a rattle.

Can you play a rattle?
Shake it s-l-o-w-l-y.
Shake it quickly.

17

Use your body

seeds

rattle-rattle

The dancer dances. The seeds rattle-rattle.

Can you shake your body and make the bells ring?

jingle-jangle
jingle-jangle

19

Listen carefully

What can you hear?
What makes that sound?

ch ch

maracas

violin

triangle

recorder

It's the maracas!

21

Index

Notes for adults

Making music provides children with an opportunity to think about sound and the different ways instruments can be played to create music. The concept of volume, rhythm, speed and pitch are introduced, and children are encouraged to think about how controlling their movements can create different sounds when they play instruments. The following Early Learning Goals are relevant to this series:

Creative development - music
* explore the different sounds of instruments and learn how sounds can be changed

Knowledge and understanding of the world
* look closely at similarities, differences, patterns and change
* show an interest in why things happen and how things work

Physical development
* respond to rhythm by means of gesture and movement
* manage body to create intended movements

This book looks at ways of creating music by shaking. It introduces different instruments that are shaken and the sounds they make. Comparisons are made between high and low, loud and quiet, fast and slow sounds.

Follow-up activities

* With their eyes closed, ask the children to identify the instruments that you play.

* Can the children use their instruments to create sound effects for different stories or nursery rhymes?

* See if the children can come up with sounds to represent different types of weather. Here are some examples that you might use: sunshine (bells), rain (a rainmaker), wind (tambourine) and a storm (gourd).